Jehovah's Witnesses

a detailed look at what they believe
& how to reach them with the gospel

Michael T. Floyd

Jehovah's Witnesses – a detailed look at what they believe & how to reach them with the gospel

Copyright © 2018 Northside Publications

Northside Publications is a ministry of Northside Baptist Church.

All Scripture quotations taken from the King James Version.

Pastor Joseph Huss
Northside Baptist Church
4601 N Division St
Davenport, IA 52806
www.northsideqc.com

ISBN 978-0-9996873-6-9

Printed in the United States of America

JEHOVAH'S WITNESSES

TABLE OF CONTENTS

INTRODUCTION
How to Determine Truth

Today many believe that all opinions and systems of beliefs are of equal value, but the Bible says, "Believe not every spirit." How do we determine truth? Is there an objective standard by which any belief system may be judged? Yes there is, and the Bible claims to be that standard.

We must use the Bible to determine truth. If we come across someone who believes differently than us, we have to ask ourselves, "Which viewpoint can be backed up by the Bible?"

Beloved, believe not every spirit, but try the spirits whether they are of God: because many false prophets are gone out into the world. Hereby know ye the Spirit of God:

7

Every spirit that confesseth that Jesus Christ is come in the flesh is of God: And every spirit that confesseth not that Jesus Christ is come in the flesh is not of God: and this is that spirit of antichrist, whereof ye have heard that it should come; and even now already is it in the world. Ye are of God, little children, and have overcome them: because greater is he that is in you, than he that is in the world.
1 John 4:1-4

The Bible commands us not to believe everything we hear – no matter how sincere the messenger. This passage tells us how to identify false prophets: What do they say about Christ? "Jesus Christ is come in the flesh" means He is the Savior (Jesus), He is the Messiah (Christ), He has fulfilled the prophecies given in the Old Testament about the Messiah, and He is God but also man (come in the flesh). He is fully human and fully God. These things are crucial to the gospel message. We must pay attention to what teachers say about Jesus. Who is Christ?

Whosoever transgresseth, and abideth not in the doctrine of Christ, hath not God. He that abideth in the doctrine of Christ,

he hath both the Father and the Son.
2 John 1:9

If you don't know Christ, you don't know God.

CHAPTER 1
Who They Are

The doorbell rings. You open the door to find a couple of people standing on your step, asking if you have a few minutes to talk. They seem gracious, sincere, and kind. They even quote a few Bible verses. As you talk with them, you find out they are Jehovah's Witnesses, and you begin to wonder: Is their message true? Does it match up with the Bible?

The purpose of this short book is to explain the beliefs of Jehovah's Witnesses and compare them to the Bible. This book is not an attack on the character of Jehovah's Witnesses. Many of them are gracious and kind, and some act more Christian than some born-again people. They are sincere, but according to the Bible, their doctrine is wrong.

THEIR ORIGIN

Jehovah's Witnesses were founded by a man named Charles Taze Russell. He claimed to be redeemed as a teenager, began teaching the Bible at age 18, and became a pastor when he was 24. His movement became known as the Watch Tower Society. After his death in 1916, Joseph Rutherford became his successor. There was a split over this decision, and those who followed Rutherford became known as Jehovah's Witnesses. Today Jehovah's Witnesses claim to have over 8 million *publishers* (those who evangelize) and over 20 million people attending their annual Memorial, which commemorates the death of Christ.[1] Their headquarters is in Warwick, New York,[2] and their current head is Robert Ciranko.[3]

JUST A MATTER OF SEMANTICS

Many religions often use the same terms as biblical Christianity but define them differently. When witnessing, you often need to ask the question, "What do you mean by that?" We must ask people to define their terminology when we talk with them. Otherwise, we may think our beliefs are the same, but they're not. For example, have you heard of The People's Republic of China? The people don't really own it, it isn't a republic, but it is China.

Differences in terminology are often dismissed as a matter of semantics. Semantics is defined as, "The branch of linguistics and logic concerned with meaning."[4] So when someone says, "It's just a matter of semantics," they are saying, "It doesn't matter what we mean." Yes, it does matter what we mean! The gospel cannot be clearly communicated unless we understand the words being used. Here is what Jehovah's Witnesses mean when they say these words:

Jehovah – An eternal being, who is the Creator of all;[5] the only true God.[6]

The Word (or the Logos) – A mighty god, but not Almighty God;[7] the beginning of God's creation.[8] John describes Jesus as the Word, so Jehovah's Witnesses believe that Jesus is a created being. Jehovah's Witnesses are polytheists. They believe in two gods: Jehovah (the supreme god) and Jesus (the lesser god).

13

The Bible – The inerrant and inspired Word of God.[9] Despite this stated belief, they have added other books that they consider to be equal with the Scriptures and interpret the Bible by these other books.

Man – Originally created in Jehovah's image[10] but then sinned and became sinners.[11] The most faithful will inherit the heavenly kingdom, others will inherit the new earth,[12] and those who reject Jehovah will be annihilated.[13]

Jesus – A mortal man[14] but resurrected as a divine spirit (no longer human).[15]

Man's Soul – Not eternal, but mortal. (It can cease to exist.)[16]

Hell – The grave. (A place of eternal torment doesn't exist.)[17]

Christ's Second Coming – Until recently, they taught that Jesus returned to earth invisibly in 1914 and is overthrowing Satan's organization and establishing the kingdom.[18] Now they teach that in 1914 Jesus was given rule of the Messianic Kingdom in Heaven, and soon His government will exercise its rule over all the earth.[19]

Trinity – A doctrine invented by Satan.[20]

Holy Spirit – Not a person, but God's active force.[21]

Redemption – Restores perfect human life.[22]

Immortality – A reward for faithfulness.[23]

144,000 – The most faithful who will be invisible, spirit creatures, just like Christ, in the heavenly kingdom.[24]

The Unrighteous – They will be resurrected in the earthly kingdom and given a chance to joyfully submit to God's rule or be annihilated.[25]

CHAPTER 2
What They Believe

In this chapter we will examine several doctrines taught by Jehovah's Witnesses and compare them to the Bible.

THE ATONEMENT

Jehovah's Witnesses claim that Christ's death "is 'a corresponding ransom for all' those who take the steps necessary to benefit from it."[26] Who can say, "I have taken all the necessary steps"? No one can say that and be honest. We have all been disobedient to God. The Bible doesn't say things like that. Jesus didn't die for the righteous or only the anointed (the faithful 144,000). He died for everybody.

And he is the propitiation for our sins: and not for ours only, but also for the sins of the whole world. 1 John 2:2

In the sight of God, there is not a good person on the earth. The Bible says, "There is none righteous, no, not one" (Romans 3:10). God looks down at mankind and sees sinners, and that is who He loves. In fact, that is who Christ died for.

But God commendeth his love toward us, in that, while we were yet sinners, Christ died for us. Romans 5:8

Christ didn't say, "Clean up your act, then I'll die for you." He said, "I'll die for you just the way you are." The old hymn, "At the Cross," says it so well: Christ died "for such a worm as I."[27] Christ died for everyone, and He is the only proper sacrifice for sins.

For by grace are ye saved through faith; and that not of yourselves: it is the gift of God: Not of works, lest any man should boast. Ephesians 2:8-9

These are the verses, especially verse 9, that convinced me to place my trust in Christ when I was 16 years old. I was raised a Presbyterian and had family in Baptist churches, Methodist churches, and Mormon churches, and I had

18

always heard that you have to be good to go to Heaven. I didn't know how good, and I didn't know if I was good enough. When I saw, "Not of works," that destroyed everything I had ever heard. I had been taught, "You've got to work for it and earn it." When these verses were pointed out to me, I thought, "I've been lied to my entire life. They've been lying to me in church." We don't need to do anything but believe.

> *But to him that worketh not, but believeth on him that justifieth the ungodly, his faith is counted for righteousness. Romans 4:5*

If you are adding works, if you believe that it is Jesus plus what you can do, then you are not trusting Christ. Your faith is in Jesus and yourself. Before I was saved, my faith was in me. I said I was a Christian, but I was trusting myself to get to Heaven. In that condition, I would've gone straight to Hell if I had died. It is not Jesus plus someone or something else; it is Jesus only.

> *Therefore we conclude that a man is justified by faith without the deeds of the law. Romans 3:28*

The Word of God says that the conclusion of the matter is that "a man is justified by faith without the deeds of the law." The conclusion is faith in Christ only.

THE DEITY OF CHRIST

As we saw earlier, Jehovah's Witnesses believe that Jesus is a mighty god, but not Almighty God. They get the term *mighty god* from Isaiah 9:6: "For unto us a child is born, unto us a son is given: and the government shall be upon his shoulder: and his name shall be called Wonderful, Counsellor, The mighty God...." They say that Jesus is a mighty god, but Jehovah is Almighty God. Jesus is some sort of lesser god that Jehovah made. Wait a minute! We just need to finish the verse: "...his name shall be called Wonderful, Counsellor, The mighty God, **The everlasting Father**, The Prince of Peace" (emphasis mine). This verse clearly states that Jesus is the Son and the Father, and He is the Father from eternity past to eternity future.

I have a son named Matthew and daughters named Dana and Sarah. I am very proud of them. I became a father at roughly 9:30 in the evening on July 23, 1976, when Matthew was born. Before that, I was not a father. I will be a father throughout eternity because we are going to live forever, but I am not an everlasting father because I became a father at a point in time. God is an everlasting Father, and this verse is talking about the Son. It is calling the Son the everlasting Father. The Son is "The mighty God, The everlasting Father."

There is unity within the Godhead – the Father, Son, and Holy Spirit. This is something we can't figure out, but God tells us to believe it. It is in the Bible, so we know it is true. To be an everlasting father, you must have an everlasting child. The Son is everlasting too. He has always been; He wasn't created.

> *In the beginning was the Word, and the Word was with God, and the Word was God. John 1:1*

This verse makes it clear that Jesus (the Word) was both with God and is God. Jehovah's Witnesses want to insert the indefinite article *a* between *was* and *God*. The Watch Tower Society has their own translation, *The New World Translation*, and they insert the word *a*. They insist that the Greek demands it be added, but that is not so. You don't have to use this verse to prove to them the Trinity or the Deity of

Christ. Using other verses is better than quibbling about translations, but they will bring this verse up. However, this passage does bring up a very important point.

> *In the beginning was the Word, and the Word was with God, and the Word was God. The same was in the beginning with God. All things were made by him; and without him was not any thing made that was made. John 1:1-3*

This verse says that Christ made everything, and that there was nothing created that wasn't made by Him. John is being very specific here. He wants us to realize that this One, the Word, who was with God and was God, is the Creator of everything in the universe. If He made everything, then He cannot be a created being as the Jehovah's Witnesses claim because you can't create yourself. It isn't possible. Jesus is not a lesser god created by Jehovah; Jesus *is* Jehovah.

> *Thus saith the LORD, thy redeemer, and he that formed thee from the womb, I am the LORD that maketh all things; that stretcheth forth the heavens alone; that spreadeth abroad the earth by myself; Isaiah 44:24*

Remember, when the word *Lord* is capitalized, *LORD*, that means Jehovah. Who does Isaiah say is the Creator? Jehovah is the Creator, but John says that Jesus is the Creator. Both Hebrews 1:2 and Colossians 1:16 say that Jesus is the Creator. Jesus and Jehovah are the same person.

When I was in Bible college, one of our teachers taught us to use what he called, "the setup technique," when talking to someone who doesn't believe in the deity of Christ. Luke 2:11 says, "For unto you is born this day in the city of David a Saviour, which is Christ the Lord." Is Jesus the Savior? Yes, this verse says that He is the Savior. A Jehovah's Witness would agree that Jesus is the Savior but not that Jesus is God. After establishing that Jesus is the Savior, show him this verse:

*I, even I, am the LORD; **and beside me there is no saviour.** Isaiah 43:11 (emphasis mine)*

If Jesus is the Savior, then Jesus has to be Jehovah. There is only one Savior and that is Jehovah, but Luke 2:11 claims that Jesus is the Savior. Either we have a contradiction, or Jesus is Jehovah.

*I am the LORD, and there is none else,
there is no God beside me: I girded thee,
though thou hast not known me:
Isaiah 45:5*

There is only one God (Jehovah); Jesus cannot be a different kind of a god because there is no other god. I encourage you to go to Zechariah 12 and begin reading from the beginning of the chapter to at least verse 10. The passage keeps saying, "the LORD, the LORD, the LORD," over and over again.

*And I [Jehovah] will pour upon the house
of David, and upon the inhabitants of Jerusalem, the spirit of grace and of supplica-
tions: and **they shall look upon me whom
they have pierced**, and they shall mourn
for him, as one mourneth for his only son,
and shall be in bitterness for him, as one
that is in bitterness for his firstborn.
Zechariah 12:10 (emphasis mine)*

When was Jehovah pierced? He was pierced at Calvary. The day is coming when Israel is going to see Jesus, and Romans tells us that they will be saved (Romans 11:26).

Jehovah's Witnesses like to say that Jesus was *begotten*, therefore, He cannot be everlasting God. He had to have a beginning; He is not from everlasting. They use verses like Psalm 2:7, "I will declare the decree: the LORD hath said unto me, Thou *art* my Son; this day have I begotten thee."

However, the apostles taught that Jesus was begotten at the resurrection – not at the birth or sometime before then.

> God hath fulfilled the same unto us their children, in that he hath raised up Jesus again; as it is also written in the second psalm, Thou art my Son, this day have I begotten thee. Acts 13:33

The prophecy by David about the Messiah being begotten was about His resurrection. He wasn't begotten in Bethlehem but at the empty tomb. When Jesus came back from the dead, He became the first-born from the dead. This is what the Bible means when it says *begotten*.

When *begotten* is used in John 3:16, it simply means, "one of a kind."[28] Some religions say, "We're all sons of God." This is not the same thing. Jesus is the everlasting Son of God; He has always been and always will be the Son of God.

> But thou, Bethlehem Ephratah, though thou be little among the thousands of

Judah, yet out of thee shall he come forth unto me that is to be ruler in Israel; whose goings forth have been from of old, from everlasting. Micah 5:2 (emphasis mine)

This is also interesting:

That at the name of Jesus every knee should bow, of things in heaven, and things in earth, and things under the earth; And that every tongue should confess that Jesus Christ is Lord, to the glory of God the Father. Philippians 2:10-11

Every knee will bow, and every tongue will confess that Jesus is Lord.

I [Jehovah] have sworn by myself, the word is gone out of my mouth in righteousness, and shall not return, That unto me every knee shall bow, every tongue shall swear. Isaiah 45:23

Jehovah said that every knee will bow and every tongue will confess to Him, and the Apostle Paul said that Jesus is the One to whom every knee will bow and every tongue will confess. Again, it is clear that Jesus is Jehovah. He was not just a good man. Was He a good man, teacher, and example? Yes, but He was more than that. He was God in the flesh who came to be our Savior.

For in him dwelleth all the fulness of the Godhead bodily. Colossians 2:9

All there is of the Father is in Jesus, and Jesus has a body. He is human, but He is the God-man. The fulness of the Godhead is in Christ.

THE ETERNAL STATE

Jehovah's Witnesses say that the soul of man is mortal and dies. By die, they mean that we sleep in the grave until the resurrection, and at the resurrection we will get a second chance: You can serve God with joy, or you can be annihilated. So what does the Bible say about soul sleep?

We are confident, I say, and willing rather to be absent from the body, and to be present with the Lord. 2 Corinthians 5:8

What happens to believers who die right now? They leave the body, go to Heaven, and are present with the Lord.

Remember the story of the rich man and Lazarus? They both died, and they both went to Hades or Sheol. (Hades is the Greek word, and Sheol is the Hebrew word.) Lazarus, who was a poor beggar, went to Abraham's bosom. There was a great gulf, and on the other side of the gulf, there was fire. That was where the rich man went. They saw each other across the gulf, and they spoke to each other. Abraham was there, so the rich man spoke to Abraham: "Can I have just a drop of water to quench my tongue?"

Abraham replied, "Sorry, but there is no way anyone can pass from here to you." It doesn't sound like they're asleep. They were fully conscious, and the rich man was in torment.

Remember when Christ died on the cross, He told the thief, "This day you will be with Me in paradise"? He was referring to Abraham's bosom in Hades. That is where the Old Testament saints went when they died. They didn't go to Heaven because their sin wasn't paid for yet. Rather, they went to paradise and stayed there until after Christ's resurrection. The lost, like the rich man, were in flames 2,000 years ago, and they still are. There is no soul sleep.

Jehovah's Witnesses claim that there is no place of torment for the dead.[29] The wicked just cease to exist. The Bible, however, states the opposite.

> *And the third angel followed them, saying with a loud voice, If any man worship the beast and his image, and receive his mark in his forehead, or in his hand, The same*

shall drink of the wine of the wrath of God, which is poured out without mixture into the cup of his indignation; and he shall be tormented with fire and brimstone in the presence of the holy angels, and in the presence of the Lamb: And the smoke of their torment ascendeth up for ever and ever: and they have no rest day nor night, who worship the beast and his image, and whosoever receiveth the mark of his name. Revelation 14:9-11

Hell is real, eternal, and it is honest-to-goodness fire. It is an awful place created for the Devil and his angels, but it is where lost people go. The Bible is very clear that everybody is going to last forever in a resurrected body. Some are resurrected to spend eternity with God, and others are resurrected to spend eternity in Hell. That is a dreadful thought, but it is true. God is just in punishing sinners, but He offers to every one of them eternal life.

Even as Sodom and Gomorrha, and the cities about them in like manner, giving themselves over to fornication, and going after strange flesh, are set forth for an example, suffering the vengeance of eternal fire. Jude 1:7

29

They have been suffering for about 4,000 years now, and it will never end.

THE HOLY SPIRIT

Jehovah's Witnesses say that the Spirit is just a force, but the Bible says that He is God.

> But Peter said, Ananias, why hath Satan filled thine heart to lie to the Holy Ghost, and to keep back part of the price of the land? Whiles it remained, was it not thine own? and after it was sold, was it not in thine own power? why hast thou conceived this thing in thine heart? thou hast not lied unto men, but unto God.
> Acts 5:3-4

Ananias and Sapphira had decided to sell their property, give some of the money to the church in Jerusalem, and claim that they gave all the money they sold it for. They wanted to be big shots in the church, but they were lying. Peter told them that they didn't lie to men, but to the Holy Spirit who is God.

> As they ministered to the Lord, and fasted, the Holy Ghost said, Separate me Barnabas and Saul for the work whereunto I have called them. So they, being sent forth by the Holy Ghost, departed unto

Seleucia; and from thence they sailed to Cyprus. Acts 13:2,4

The Holy Spirit can speak. A force doesn't speak; you have to be a person to articulate words. The Spirit also sent them out. The Spirit of God can speak, and He can send out missionaries. He has to be a Person. He is not an it or a thing; He is not something you feel, like when you stand in front of a fireplace and feel the heat. Fire is a force or energy; the fireplace can't talk to you. The fire cannot send out missionaries because it has no intelligence. It can't think, reason, or do things. The Spirit of God can do those things because He is a Person.

And grieve not the holy Spirit of God, whereby ye are sealed unto the day of redemption. Ephesians 4:30

By living the wrong kind of life, a Christian can grieve the Holy Spirit. The Spirit is a Person who can be grieved by others' choices. He has emotions. When you insult Him, He feels it. He lives within those of us who have placed our trust in Jesus. We shouldn't grieve or quench Him.

But all these worketh that one and the selfsame Spirit, dividing to every man severally as he will. 1 Corinthians 12:11

This passage is talking about spiritual gifts and lists many of the gifts. This verse says that the Holy Spirit gives these gifts according to His will. A force has no will. For example, let's use heat energy. Men can capture heat energy and use it for various purposes, such as your car. There is an explosion in the cylinder and that heat energy drives the piston down. When the engine keeps cranking like that, it moves your car down the road. Although the energy is moving the car, it doesn't have a will. A man who has a will figured out how to capture that energy and put it to work. It takes a person.

The Spirit is a Person because He decides things, including the spiritual gifts you have received. You don't get to decide your gifts; the Spirit decides. It is our duty to submit and then use the gifts we have been given.

The Father, the Son, and the Spirit are all Persons, and they are all God, but there is only one God. The Bible makes it very clear that there is only one God but that there are three Persons in the Godhead.

THE HUMANITY OF CHRIST

And the Word was made flesh, and dwelt among us, (and we beheld his glory, the glory as of the only begotten of the Father,) full of grace and truth. John 1:14

Jesus had a body. There are people who claim that Jesus didn't have a body, and Jehovah's Witnesses claim He doesn't have a body now. In the first century, there was a group of people who said that Jesus wasn't really human; He just appeared human. These people were known as Gnostics.

That which was from the beginning, which we have heard, which we have seen with our eyes, which we have looked upon, and our hands have handled, of the Word of life; (For the life was manifested, and we have seen it, and bear witness, and shew unto you that eternal life, which was with the Father, and was manifested unto us;) That which we have seen and heard declare we unto you, that ye also may have fellowship with us: and truly our fellowship is with the Father, and with his Son Jesus Christ. 1 John 1:1-3

We know from John 1 that Jesus is the Word. John is being very specific in 1 John 1 when he says that they heard Him, saw Him, examined Him, and handled Him. He was real, and He was definitely human. He tells us this so we can have fellowship with God and each other. God wants us to walk with Him. He wants a real relationship with us, and He wants us to enjoy His company. This is possible because of the God-man. He was really human and really God at the same time – and still is.

THE ONE HUNDRED FORTY-FOUR THOUSAND

There are millions of Jehovah's Witnesses, and many of them would like to be part of the 144,000.

> And I heard the number of them which were sealed: and there were sealed an hundred and forty and four thousand of all the tribes of the children of Israel. Of the tribe of Juda were sealed twelve thousand. Of the tribe of Reuben were sealed twelve thousand. Of the tribe of Gad were sealed twelve thousand. Of the tribe of Aser were sealed twelve thousand. Of the tribe of Nepthalim were sealed twelve thousand. Of the tribe of Manasses were sealed twelve thousand. Of the tribe of

Simeon were sealed twelve thousand. Of the tribe of Levi were sealed twelve thousand. Of the tribe of Issachar were sealed twelve thousand. Of the tribe of Zabulon were sealed twelve thousand. Of the tribe of Joseph were sealed twelve thousand. Of the tribe of Benjamin were sealed twelve thousand. Revelation 7:4-8

The 144,000 are not American Jehovah's Witnesses; they are Jewish. John is very specific in describing this group. There are 12,000 from each of the twelve tribes.

And I looked, and, lo, a Lamb stood on the mount Sion, and with him an hundred forty and four thousand, having his Father's name written in their foreheads. And I heard a voice from heaven, as the voice of many waters, and as the voice of a great thunder: and I heard the voice of harpers harping with their harps: And they sung as it were a new song before the throne, and before the four beasts, and the elders: and no man could learn that song but the hundred and forty and four thousand, which were redeemed from the earth. Revelation 14:1-3

This prophecy will be fulfilled during the Tribulation. These 144,000 Jews will be in Heaven. They will have been martyred for their faith.

> *These are they which were not defiled with women; for they are virgins. These are they which follow the Lamb whithersoever he goeth. These were redeemed from among men, being the firstfruits unto God and to the Lamb. Revelation 14:4*

They're Jewish, and they're unmarried men. There are a lot of Jehovah's Witness women who are hoping to be part of the 144,000, but they can't because they're neither Jewish nor unmarried men. No matter how good they are, they can't be one of them. This idea is a false teaching that one of the early leaders in the Watch Tower Society came up with that doesn't make any sense. They teach that only the 144,000 go to Heaven, but the Bible says that only Jewish men will be part of the 144,000.

What does the Bible actually say about what is going to happen to true believers?

> *But I would not have you to be ignorant, brethren, concerning them which are asleep, that ye sorrow not, even as others which have no hope. For if we believe that*

Jesus died and rose again, even so them also which sleep in Jesus will God bring with him. 1 Thessalonians 4:13-14

Does this passage teach soul sleep? No, it doesn't. Asleep just means that they have died. Where are those who are asleep? They're with God! This verse is another proof of the deity of Christ because Christ is the one who is coming back with the saints. Then it continues:

For this we say unto you by the word of the Lord, that we which are alive and remain unto the coming of the Lord shall not prevent [or precede] them which are asleep. For the Lord himself shall descend from heaven with a shout, with the voice of the archangel, and with the trump of God: and the dead in Christ shall rise first. 1 Thessalonians 4:15-16

These saints died, and their bodies were left behind, but they are with the Lord (2 Corinthians 5:8). When Christ returns, He is going to bring them with Him. Their bodies will be raised and will be reunited with their spirits in the air. Then those of us who are still alive at that time will be caught up to meet them in the air.

Then we which are alive and remain shall be caught up together with them in

the clouds, to meet the Lord in the air:
and so shall we ever be with the Lord.
1 Thessalonians 4:17 (emphasis mine)

It says that we will be with the Lord forever! We will go to Heaven for seven years and enjoy the Marriage Supper of the Lamb. While we are in Heaven, the Tribulation will be going on down here on earth. Then we will return with Him for the Battle of Armageddon and the 1,000 year reign of Christ on the earth. At that time, we will be ruling with Him in the prophesied Kingdom – not just the 144,000. After the 1,000 years, the old Heaven and earth will pass away, and there will be a new Heaven and new earth. God will send down the New Jerusalem from Heaven to the new earth. Christ will be there, and we will be with Him forever and ever.

THE PHYSICAL RESURRECTION OF CHRIST

A very important doctrine that Jehovah's Witnesses get wrong is their teaching of the resurrection. They say that Jesus was resurrected as an invisible spirit. They claim that Christ did *not* have a bodily resurrection, but rather His body disappeared.[30] Believing in the bodily resurrection of Jesus is crucial for believing the gospel. There are many others who don't believe in the bodily resurrection of Christ either. Many mainstream Protestant preachers say that Jesus had a spiritual resurrection. I'm not sure what a spiritual resurrection is. If the body hasn't come out of the grave, you haven't had a resurrection. It's that simple.

> *Jesus answered and said unto them, Destroy this temple, and in three days I will raise it up. Then said the Jews, Forty and six years was this temple in building, and wilt thou rear it up in three days? But he spake of the temple of **his body**.*
> *John 2:19-21 (emphasis mine)*

Jesus predicted that He would have a physical resurrection. If they destroyed His body, He would come back in His body in three days, and that is exactly what He did. It was a physical resurrection. After the resurrection, Christ demonstrated that He had a body.

> *Behold my hands and my feet, that it is I myself: handle me, and see; for a spirit hath not flesh and bones, as ye see me have. Luke 24:39*

Christ basically said, "Look at me; touch me. I've got a body; I'm not a spirit!" This example makes it very clear that there are many people in the world who claim to believe the Bible, but the truth is they don't. How can Christ get any clearer than this? He can't! He had a literal body of flesh and bones.

He still has a body, and He will always have one.

> Who shall change our vile body, that it may be fashioned like unto his glorious body, according to the working whereby he is able even to subdue all things unto himself. Philippians 3:21

Christ came back from the dead and ascended up to Heaven. He has been glorified and now has a glorious body. Revelation 1 describes how Christ looks today, but He still has a body.

The Jehovah's Witnesses use the story of the disciples on the road to Emmaus to show that Christ did not have a body because they didn't recognize him. The fact that they didn't recognize Him doesn't prove He didn't have a body. In Luke 24:16, it says that "their eyes were holden that they should not know him." The problem wasn't with Christ's body; the problem was with their sight. God, for reasons of His own, at that point kept them from recognizing Him, but before it was over, they did recognize Him.

THE PHYSICAL RETURN OF CHRIST

As I mentioned earlier, Israel will see Him "whom they have pierced." Christ still bears the marks of Calvary. The piercings are still there. We will see them on His body, and I believe that He will bear them for all eternity as a remembrance of what He did for us. The Bible is clear that when Christ returns, He is going to have a body.

> *Behold, he cometh with clouds; and every eye shall see him, and they also which pierced him: and all kindreds of the earth shall wail because of him. Even so, Amen. Revelation 1:7*

If Jesus is an invisible spirit, then how will every eye see Him? Jesus is not an invisible spirit; Christ is coming again in the same physical body He ascended in.

THE TRINITY

Jehovah's Witnesses love to say that the word *Trinity* is not in the Bible. That is true. The word *Bible* is not in the Bible either. There are a lot of words that you won't find in the Bible. In reality, you won't find *Jehovah* in the Bible. In the ancient Hebrew, *Jehovah* was made up of four letters with no vowels, and the Jewish people wouldn't pronounce it. We have no idea how the word is pronounced. Somewhere down the ages, somebody decided *Jehovah* sounded good, and I am fine with that. There are others who say *Yahweh*, and that is fine too because nobody knows how it is pronounced. Just because a word isn't found in the Bible doesn't mean that the doctrine isn't in there. That is what we see with the doctrine of the Trinity.

> *Hear, O Israel: The LORD our God is one LORD: Deuteronomy 6:4*

Without a doubt, God is one. The Hebrew word for *one* means, "a composite unity"[31] not a single or solitary being. Whenever you see *LORD* in the King James Version, that is Jehovah. The verse is saying, "Jehovah our Elohim is one Jehovah." The word *Elohim* is a plural word. Hebrew has singular (one), dual (two), or plural (three or more). This verse shows that Jehovah (singular) is one Elohim (plural; we know from Scripture that it is three). He is one, but there are three persons in the one God. They are not three separate gods, but one God. The same word for *one* is used in Genesis 2:24: "Therefore shall a man leave his father and his mother, and shall cleave unto his wife: and they shall be **one** flesh" (emphasis mine). In this example, *one* is a composite of two. There are two people who become one flesh in the sight of God.

Deuteronomy 6:4 does not discredit the doctrine of the Trinity by saying that God is one LORD. That is not what the word means. God is one, but in that oneness, there are different members.

> *And God said, Let **us** make man in our **image**, after **our** likeness: and let them have dominion over the fish of the sea, and over the fowl of the air, and over the cattle, and over all the earth, and over every creeping thing that creepeth upon the earth. So God created man in **his own image**, in the image of God created he him; male and female created he them. Genesis 1:26-27 (emphasis mine)*

If you quote verse 26 to a Jehovah's Witness, he'll say that God was talking to the angels. No, He wasn't; God was talking to Himself. God created man in His own image, and He said, "Our" and "Us."

*I am the LORD, and there is none else,
there is no God beside me: I girded thee,
though thou hast not known me:
Isaiah 45:5*

There is only one God. Jehovah's Witnesses say that Jesus is a mighty god, but not Almighty God. Jesus can't be a different type of god because the Bible says that there is only one God. If Jesus is God at all, which He is, then He and the Father have to be joined together somehow.

Jesus was baptized in the Jordan river by John. When Jesus came out of the water, the Holy Spirit descended like a dove, and the Father spoke from Heaven and said, "This is my beloved Son, in whom I am well pleased" (Matthew 3:17). All three members of the Trinity were there at the same time. Some people claim that there is only one person of the Godhead, but sometimes He appears as the Father, the Son, or the Holy Spirit. That is not true; He is all three at once, but there is only one God. There are three persons but one being or essence.

In the Great Commission, Christ gives us the baptismal formula. Matthew 28:19 says, "Go ye therefore, and teach all nations, baptizing them in the name of the Father, and of the Son, and of the Holy Ghost." Notice it says, "In the name" (singular). There is only one God, but three persons.

Can I absolutely, positively understand it all? No. Do I have to comprehend it? Why? If I could understand God, I don't think He could be God anymore. There are things that are beyond our comprehension. The world doesn't like to admit that, but it is the truth. There are many things that we don't know. I really believe that there is a Being who created this entire universe, who is beyond my comprehension. I don't have a problem with that. There are a lot of things I have a hard time understanding; I had a hard time in Algebra. My ability to comprehend something doesn't make it true or false. If the Bible says it, I believe it.

> For there are three that bear record in heaven, the Father, the Word, and the Holy Ghost: and these three are one.
> 1 John 5:7

CHAPTER 3
How to Reach Them

When you answer your door and there are a couple of Jehovah's Witnesses there, be kind to them. Don't be nasty. If you're mean, they just become more persuaded that they're right and everybody else is wrong.

One thing I realized from doing door-to-door evangelism myself is that we must be kind, but we must not aid the spreading of a false gospel. There were times in the winter when I was thinking, "If somebody doesn't let me in soon, I will have to go home because I am freezing to death." My pen had frozen a long while before, and I wasn't able to fill out the survey form. Well, when someone with a false gospel comes to your door in that situation, they're thinking the same thing. Do you want to let them in your door and enable them to go on another hour or two?

Be nice and witness to them, but grab your coat and get out there on your doorstep. Don't give aid and comfort to someone who is spreading a false gospel. The same thing applies in the summer; don't offer them a glass of iced tea. I'm not saying be unkind. However, if they go down the street and convince one of your neighbors that they're right, and they would've gone home if you didn't let them in to warm up or cool down, then you become a partaker in sharing a false gospel. You don't want to give account for that.

> If there come any unto you, and bring not this doctrine, receive him not into your house, neither bid him God speed: For he that biddeth him God speed is partaker of his evil deeds. 2 John 1:10-11

You might not be able to use much of the information offered in this book when witnessing to a Jehovah's Witness. If you know somebody, these are things you may get to share if they allow you to, but in your average witnessing opportunity with a Jehovah's Witness, you won't get to talk all that much, so give them the gospel. Try not to let them leave your doorstep without telling them that God loves them, He sent His Son to die and pay for their sin, He was raised from the dead, and He is able and willing to save their souls.

If you come across someone from any religion who has questions that you never imagined anyone would ever ask, what do you do? Give them the gospel! That is how they get saved, hearing and then believing the gospel.

When I was in Bible college, I was passing out tracts at a beach in Florida. I stopped and talked to a couple. The guy was kind of interested, but the girl said that she had given up religion years ago. Her problem was that she was raised in a legalistic environment where she had to do all of these things to hope to get to Heaven. She couldn't do all of those things, and she probably didn't want to do all of those things, so she said, "I don't believe in God." I gave her the gospel, and she trusted Christ!

Give people the gospel; that is what you should be an expert on. You don't have to be an expert on each and every religion. In any religion, except for true Christianity, you have to work for some kind of salvation. That is the number one difference between Christianity and other religions. Christianity is the grace of God saving sinners, but every other religion is being good and working to save your own soul. You don't need to know everything that Jehovah's Witnesses believe. It can be helpful to be able to answer some of their questions, but the main thing is to know the gospel and to be able to give it clearly.

Jesus is God who gave Himself as the sacrifice for sin. No one can go to Heaven by being a good Baptist, Catholic, Presbyterian, Methodist, Lutheran, Mormon, or Jehovah's Witness. You cannot go to Heaven by being a good religious person because you cannot go to Heaven by being good. You can only get to Heaven through the sacrifice of Jesus Christ. He died for you, He paid for your sin, He was raised from the dead, He is alive, and He says that the Father has given Him the power to give life to those who would believe in Him. Put your faith in Christ, and He'll give you everlasting life.

ENDNOTES

[1]"2017 Grand Totals," Watch Tower Bible and Tract Society of Pennsylvania, 2018, jw.org/en/publications/books/2017-service-year-report/2017-grand-totals

[2]"Nearly 400 Attend Open House at Jehovah's Witnesses' New World Headquarters," Watch Tower Bible and Tract Society of Pennsylvania, 2017, jw.org/en/news/releases/by-region/united-states/open-house-new-world-headquarters-jehovahs-witnesses

[3]"Warning Issued to Witnesses' Headquarters in Russia Threatens Religious Freedom," Watch Tower Bible and Tract Society of Pennsylvania,

2016, jw.org/en/news/legal/by-region/russia/jw-religious-freedom-threatened

[4]*Oxford Dictionary*, semantics, Oxford University Press, 2018, en.oxforddictionaries.com/definition/semantics

[5]"Did God Have a Beginning?" *The Watchtower*, Watch Tower Bible and Tract Society of Pennsylvania, July 2010

[6]"Is There Only One True God?" *Awake*, Watch Tower Bible and Tract Society of Pennsylvania, February 2006

[7]*The Truth Shall Make You Free*, p. 47, Watchtower Bible and Tract Society, 1943

[8]*The Kingdom Is at Hand*, pp. 46-47, Watchtower Bible and Tract Society, 1944

[9]"Inspiration," *Insight on the Scriptures*, Volume 1, pp.1202-1207, Watch Tower Bible and Tract Society of Pennsylvania, 1988

[10]"Become Imitators of God," *The Watchtower*, Watch Tower Bible and Tract Society of Pennsylvania, October 2008

[11]"Why Do People Die?" Watch Tower Bible and Tract Society of Pennsylvania, 2018, jw.org/en/bible-teachings/questions/why-do-people-die

[12]"Do All Good People Go to Heaven?" *The Watchtower*, Watch Tower Bible and Tract Society of Pennsylvania, February 2010

[13]"Will Bad People Burn in Hell?" *Awake*, Watch Tower Bible and Tract Society of Pennsylvania, September 2009

[14]*Let God Be True*, p. 71, Watchtower Bible and Tract Society, 1946

[15]*The Kingdom Is at Hand*, pp. 258, Watchtower Bible and Tract Society, 1944

[16]"What Is the Soul?" Watch Tower Bible and Tract Society of Pennsylvania, 2018, jw.org/en/bible-teachings/questions/what-is-a-soul

[17]"Who Goes to Hell?" Watch Tower Bible and Tract Society of Pennsylvania, 2018, jw.org/en/bible-teachings/questions/who-goes-to-hell

[18]*The Kingdom, The Hope of the World*, p.8, Watchtower Bible & Tract Society, 1931

[19]"When Will God's Kingdom Come?" *The Watchtower*, Watch Tower Bible and Tract Society of Pennsylvania, January 2008

[20]*Let God Be True*, p.101, Watchtower Bible and Tract Society, 1946

[21]*Let God Be True*, p.108, Watchtower Bible and Tract Society, 1946

[22]*Let God Be True*, p.114, Watchtower Bible and Tract Society, 1946

[23]*Let God Be True*, p.74, Watchtower Bible and Tract Society, 1946

[24]"Grafting from the Wild Olive Tree," *The Watchtower*, Watch Tower Bible and Tract Society of Pennsylvania, March 1958

[25]"What Hope for My Ancestors?" *The Watchtower*, Watch Tower Bible and Tract Society of Pennsylvania, June 2014

[26]"How Is Jesus' Sacrifice 'a Ransom for Many'?" Watch Tower Bible and Tract Society of Pennsylvania, 2018, jw.org/en/bible-teachings/questions/jesus-sacrifice-ransom/

[27]Isaac Watts and Ralph E. Hudson, "At the Cross," 1885

[28]Andreas J. Köstenberger and Scott R. Swain, *Father, Son, and Spirit*, p. 77, InterVarsity Press, 2008

[29]"Who Goes to Hell?" Watch Tower Bible and Tract Society of Pennsylvania, 2018, jw.org/en/bible-teachings/questions/who-goes-to-hell

[30] "Jesus Is Alive," *My Book of Bible Stories*, Story 102, Watch Tower Bible and Tract Society of Pennsylvania, 2004

[31] Matt Stick, "Does Deuteronomy 6:4, the Shema, disprove the Trinity?" Christian Apologetics & Research Ministry, carm.org/questions/about-god/does-deuteronomy-64-shema-disprove-trinity

Made in the USA
Middletown, DE
14 October 2018